**THIS BOOK BELONGS TO:**

..............................................................................

TO EMMA,
MERRY CHRISTMAS!

1

To my wife and daughter, without your love and support this book would not have happened.
I love you both.

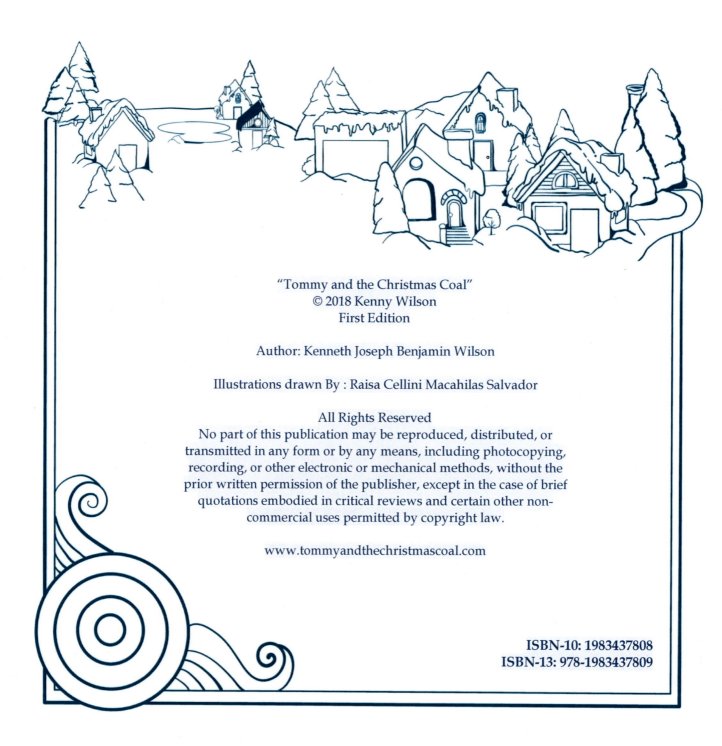

"Tommy and the Christmas Coal"
© 2018 Kenny Wilson
First Edition

Author: Kenneth Joseph Benjamin Wilson

Illustrations drawn By : Raisa Cellini Macahilas Salvador

www.tommyandthechristmascoal.com

ISBN-10: 1983437808
ISBN-13: 978-1983437809

# Tommy
## and the Christmas Coal

### By: Kenny Wilson

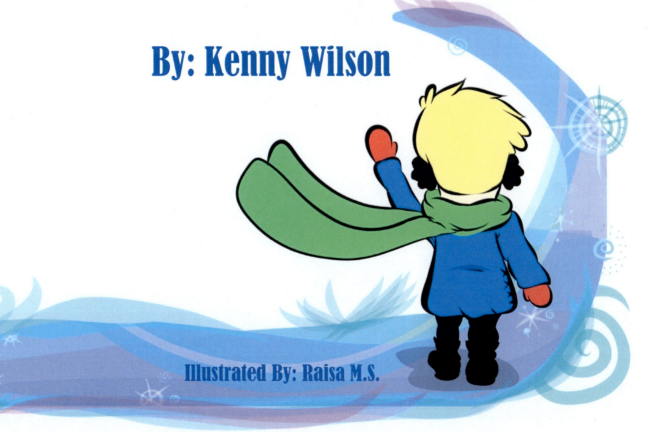

### Illustrated By: Raisa M.S.

Once upon a time, many Christmases ago
there lived a little boy named Tommy. He was one of
the most well-behaved children in his small village. He
lived at home with his mother and father in a little
house near the edge of town.

Tommy and his parents didn't have much. What they did have was a roof over their head, food in their bellies, and the love they shared for each other. Every night they would laugh and giggle while they ate vegetable soup.

Winter had settled in the little village that
Tommy lived in. The cold wind would howl at night
threatening to nip at Tommy's toes. Only a nugget of
coal burning in the stove at night would keep the cold
away as the family slept snug in their beds.

Just a week before Christmas, Tommy's father came home with sad news. Tommy's father had lost his job. The family would not be able to buy any more coal this winter. After counting their coal, they saw they only had enough to last until Christmas morning.

The next morning at school, Tommy
and his friends sat on the floor as their teacher,
Mr. Johnson began to tell them of Santa Claus. He had a
round belly and a warm smile.

He would visit the good children on
Christmas Eve to deliver presents. The bad children
however would receive a lump of coal. The worst the
children behaved, the more coal they would discover in
their stockings on Christmas morning.

Tommy spent the entire day at school thinking about Santa and the coal. He wondered if it could be true that Santa would deliver coal to a naughty boy.

He decided the only way to be sure was to ask a kid who was already on the naughty list.

Murray Sanders was the meanest boy in the class. He even took Tommy's yoyo on the first day of the school year. Tommy's knees shook as he walked across the schoolyard to Murray and tapped him on the shoulder. "Um…. Murray… Did you get coal for Christmas last year?"

Tommy winced as Murray spun around. Nothing could
have prepared him for what happened next. Murray
started to cry. All Murray could do was nod between
sobs. Finally, he composed himself and said,
"Yes. *sniff* I got coal.  All I ever get is coal."

23

"It's okay, Murray. Santa doesn't want to give you coal. Why I bet if you start being good you might even be able to get a present this Christmas," he consoled him.

Murray smiled widely. He gave Tommy his yoyo back; he would start over as a good boy from that moment on.

That night Tommy couldn't sleep. He was excited with the idea of having a coal delivery from Santa on Christmas morning for his family. There was only one problem. He didn't know how to be bad!

When Tommy woke up the next morning, he remembered that he had a test. He planned to keep his big coat on, so he could hide his school book inside.
He would cheat on his test when
Mr. Johnson wasn't looking.
That would get him on the naughty list for sure!

When he got to school though, Mr. Johnson surprised everyone. It was an open book test!!
How was Tommy going to be able to cheat when he was already allowed to look in his school book? He was so sad that his plan didn't work.

Next, Tommy saw an old shed behind Mrs. Thomas' house.  He thought he could get on the naughty list if he painted a picture on the side of her old shed. He often heard adults complaining about those graffiti pictures.

When no one was looking, Tommy snuck over to
Mrs. Thomas' house. He started painting on her shed.
He decided to make something nice instead of one of those
ugly graffiti pictures he had seen. The hours melted away
as he worked on his masterpiece.

It was beautiful.

37

After he was done, Tommy stood back to look at his painting. He hadn't noticed that Mrs. Thomas was standing right beside him with tears in her eyes and…

... a great big smile.

"It is beautiful Tommy. This is the nicest thing anyone has ever done for me," she said.

What happened next was absolutely shocking. Mrs. Thomas had been trying to get her shed painted for years.

Once the village heard about what Tommy had done, he became the town hero for the year. People began to paint each other's houses to celebrate how good Tommy was.

Christmas Eve finally arrived. Poor Tommy was devastated. No matter how hard he tried to be naughty, everything he did backfired. His Mommy saw how sad he was and gave him a big hug.

"Christmas miracles do happen Tommy. Chin up, it will be ok," she told him.

45

Tommy smiled, and wiped a tear away. At least he had the love of his family. After a dinner of vegetable soup, his family put the last piece of coal in the stove. They sang Christmas carols around the stove before going to bed.

The next morning, Tommy awoke to find a wonderful surprise.

His stocking was overflowing with coal! There was enough coal there to heat their home until next Christmas.

On his stocking there was a note from Santa, It read:

DEAR TOMMY,

YOU ARE A VERY GOOD LITTLE BOY.
WHILE IT IS HIGHLY UNUSUAL TO GIVE COAL
TO GOOD BOYS ON CHRISTMAS,
I THINK THAT WE CAN MAKE AN EXCEPTION FOR YOU.

MERRY CHRISTMAS, SANTA

The next day, all of Tommy's friends got together to talk about what Santa gave them for Christmas. Even Murray Sanders was there with a shiny new toy truck and his own yoyo. When it was Tommy's turn, he said with a huge smile, "Santa brought me coal."

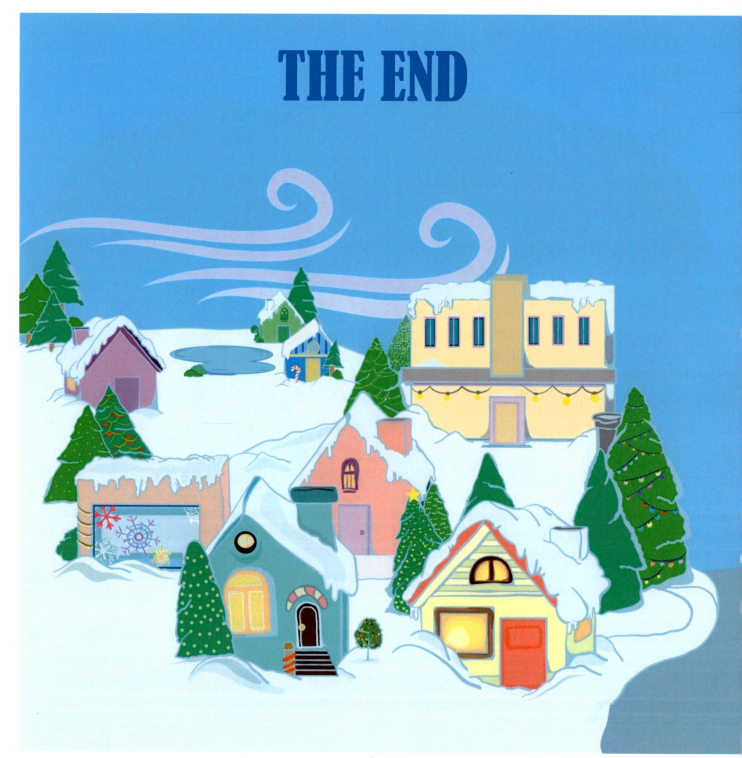

Made in the USA
Columbia, SC
23 October 2018